竞赛套路

THE COMPETITION ROUTINE OF 42 STYLE TAI JI JIAN

主　编／张　山　　Chief Editor / Zhang Shan
执行主编／武　冬　　Executive Editor / Wu Dong
英文主编／李　伟　　Editor of English Version / Li Wei

山西科学技术出版社

图书在版编目(CIP)数据

42式太极剑竞赛套路/张山等主编.—太原：山西科学技术出版社,2003.3
(太极拳竞赛套路中英对照学练指导丛书)
ISBN 7-5377-2087-8

Ⅰ.4… Ⅱ.张… Ⅲ.剑术(武术),四十二式—运动竞赛—套路(武术)—汉、英 Ⅳ.G852.241.9

中国版本图书馆 CIP 数据核字(2002)第 089683 号

42式太极剑竞赛套路

作　者：主　编：张　山
　　　　　执行主编：武　冬
　　　　　英文主编：李　伟
出版发行：山西科学技术出版社
社　　址：太原市建设南路15号
邮　　编：030012
编辑部电话：0351-4922135
发行部电话：0351-4922121
E-mail：sxkjcbs@public.ty.sx.cn
　　　　info@sxstph.com.cn
网　　址：http://www.sxstph.com.cn
印　　刷：山西新华印业有限公司人民印刷分公司
开　　本：850×1168　1/32
字　　数：106千字
印　　张：4.75
版　　次：2003年3月第一版
印　　次：2003年3月第一次印刷
印　　数：1—5000册
书　　号：ISBN 7-5377-2087-8/Z·398
定　　价：16.80元

如发现印、装质量问题，影响阅读，请与发行部联系调换。

编委会名单

主　　编 / 张　山
执行主编 / 武　冬
英文主编 / 李　伟

Chief Editor / Zhang Shan
Executive Editor / Wu Dong
Editor of English Version / Li Wei

编 委　张　山　武　冬　赵国庆　张小欧　梁小葵　王晓燕

翻 译　李　伟　黄正麟　姜安安　伍军红　武　冬　杨慧馨

Editors	Zhang Shan	Wu Dong	Zhao Guoqing
	Zhang Xiaoou	Liang Xiaokui	Wang Xiaoyan
Translated by	Li Wei	Huang Zhenglin	Jiang Anan
	Wu Junhong	Wu Dong	Yang Huixin

前　言

太极拳是一项让世界人民着迷的具有丰富内涵的运动。自从面世以来，就以其独特的运动形式、深邃的文化底蕴、显著的健身效果吸引着越来越多的人们，特别是 21 世纪的到来，在高度文明、现代化的生活中，人们渴望自然、和谐的生活，健康、结实的体魄，太极拳恰好就是实现这些愿望绝好的运动。也正是因为如此，太极拳以其特有的方式发展着，从邓小平题词"太极拳好"到天安门万人太极拳表演，从城市到乡村，从中国到世界各地，到处都可以看到众多的太极拳习练者。现在，没有人能精确地计算出世界上到底有多少人在习练太极拳，世界上到底有多少个太极拳组织。然而，太极拳已经发展到世界每一个角落，阔步天下，是人所共知的。可是，由于种种原因，众多太极拳习练者往往因为没有好的教材而哀叹，特别是对世界各地的太极拳爱好者来说更是如此。太极拳竞赛套路是由国家颁布的一个规范的系列竞赛套路，同时也是一套健身的好教材。目前已经在中国乃至世界范围内推广开来。为了更好地配合世界各地的太极拳爱好者学好练好竞赛套路，我们特推出一套完整的、中英文对照的学练太极拳竞赛套路的指导丛书，以满足广大太极拳爱好者的需求。该丛书从学练太极拳的角度出发，高度概括出了行之有效的学练程序和手段，以简洁明快的语言直指动作的核心，大量的图解照片让您能无师自通。不仅如此,我们还随书配带光盘,为您提供动态的学练环境。书和光盘中的动作示范者均为有相当水准的太极拳教练。这您一看便知,我们的目的只有一个,就是献给广大读者一个精品。

尽管我们很努力,书中仍难免有错误之处,恳请广大读者多多指正!

愿太极拳带给您一生的快乐和健康!

愿我们的这套书对您能有所帮助!

编 者

Preface

Tai Ji Quan, which captivates the people all over the world, is a sports with rich connotations. Ever since it is introduced to the world, it attracts more and more people with the unique forms, the profound cultural characteristics and the remarkable affection on people's health. In the high civilized and modern 21 century, people seek for a more natural and harmonious life and a strong and healthy physique which are the function and purpose of Tai Ji Quan. And just because of these, Tai Ji Quan is developing fast on its own way from Deng Xiao – ping's inscription "Tai Ji Quan is good" to the demonstration done by 10 000 people in Tian An Men Square, from the cities to the countries and from China to the other countries in the world. Nobody can tell exactly how many people are learning and practicing Tai Ji Quan and how many organizations of Jai Ji Quan there are in the world. Unfortunately, the participants feel sorry and disappointed for not having a good and practicable book for them to follow, especially for those foreigners who know little about Chinese and Chinese Wu Shu. The competition routine of Tai Ji Quan is issued and standardized by the nation for the purpose of the competition and keeping fit which becomes quite popular both in China and in the world. In order to help the participants all over the world for learning and practicing this routine, we present this series of guide which is a Chinese - English bilingual edition to meet your needs. This series illustrate the easy and effective ways and procedures for learning and practicing Tai Ji Quan and points out the key techniques of the movements with simple and lively words together with the tremendous photographs. In addition, we also provide you the VCDs in which you can watch and follow the demonstrations done by the famous coaches. To present you an excellency is the only purpose of this series.

Although we try hard to avoid mistakes, we may have something that are not appropriate in this book and we sincerely hope that you can help us to find out.

May Tai Ji Quan bring you happiness and health!

May this series meet your needs!

Editor

目　录

1. 42式太极剑竞赛套路简介 …………………………………（1）
   1.1 套路结构特点 …………………………………………（2）
   1.2 技术风格特点 …………………………………………（3）
2. 42式太极剑竞赛套路核心技术学练 ………………………（5）
   2.1 太极剑桩功练习 ………………………………………（6）
   2.2 核心技术动作练习 ……………………………………（10）
3. 42式太极剑竞赛套路动作图解及要点 ……………………（15）
   3.1 预备势 …………………………………………………（16）
   3.2 起势 ……………………………………………………（17）
   3.3 并步点剑 ………………………………………………（22）
   3.4 弓步斜削 ………………………………………………（25）
   3.5 提膝劈剑 ………………………………………………（27）
   3.6 左弓步拦 ………………………………………………（29）
   3.7 左虚步撩 ………………………………………………（30）
   3.8 右弓步撩 ………………………………………………（31）
   3.9 提膝捧剑 ………………………………………………（34）
   3.10 蹬脚前刺 ……………………………………………（36）
   3.11 跳步平刺 ……………………………………………（37）
   3.12 转身下刺 ……………………………………………（40）
   3.13 弓步平斩 ……………………………………………（42）
   3.14 弓步崩剑 ……………………………………………（44）
   3.15 歇步压剑 ……………………………………………（45）
   3.16 进步绞剑 ……………………………………………（48）

3.17	提膝上刺	(50)
3.18	虚步下截	(52)
3.19	右左平带	(54)
3.20	弓步劈剑	(56)
3.21	丁步托剑	(58)
3.22	分脚后点	(60)
3.23	仆步穿剑	(64)
3.24	蹬脚架剑	(66)
3.25	提膝点剑	(68)
3.26	仆步横扫	(69)
3.27	右左弓步下截	(70)
3.28	弓步下刺	(73)
3.29	右左云抹	(75)
3.30	右弓步劈	(79)
3.31	后举腿架剑	(81)
3.32	丁步点剑	(82)
3.33	马步推剑	(83)
3.34	独立上托	(84)
3.35	进步挂点	(86)
3.36	歇步崩剑	(88)
3.37	弓步反刺	(90)
3.38	转身下刺	(92)
3.39	提膝提剑	(94)
3.40	行步穿剑	(96)
3.41	摆腿架剑	(98)
3.42	弓步直刺	(101)
3.43	收势	(102)
附录1	整个套路动作路线图	(105)

附录2　学练太极拳竞赛套路指南 ……………………………………（107）

Contents

1. A Brief Introduction to the Competition Routine of 42 Style Tai Ji Jian ·················· (1)
   1.1 The Characteristics in the Structure of the Routine ·················· (2)
   1.2 The Characteristics in the Technique of the Routine ·················· (3)
2. Learning and Practicing the Key Techniques of the Competition Routine of 42 Style Tai Ji Jian ·················· (5)
   2.1 The Exercises of Tai Ji Jian Zhuang Gong ·········· (6)
   2.2 The Exercises of the Key Technical Movements ·················· (10)
3. Photographs and Key Points of the Movements of the Competition Routine of 42 Style Tai Ji Jian ·················· (15)
   3.1 Yu Bei Shi (Preparing form) ·················· (16)
   3.2 Qi Shi (Commencing form) ·················· (17)
   3.3 Bing Bu Dian Jian (Stand with feet together and point sword) ·················· (22)
   3.4 Gong Bu Xie Xiao (Bow stance and cut obliquely) ·················· (25)
   3.5 Ti Xi Pi Jian (Lift knee and chop sword) ·········· (27)
   3.6 Zuo Gong Bu Lan (Left bow stance and parry sword) ·················· (29)
   3.7 Zuo Xu Bu Liao (Left empty stance and cut upward sword) ·················· (30)

3.8　You Gong Bu Liao(Right bow stance and cut upward with sword) ………………………… (31)
3.9　Ti Xi Peng Jian(Lift knee and hold sword in both hands) ………………………………… (34)
3.10　Deng Jiao Qian Ci(Heel kick and thrust sword) ………………………………………… (36)
3.11　Tiao Bu Ping Ci(Jump step and thrust sword) ………………………………………… (37)
3.12　Zhuan Shen Xia Ci(Turn body and thrust down) ……………………………………… (40)
3.13　Gong Bu Ping Zhan(Bow stance and cut horizontally) ………………………………… (42)
3.14　Gong Bu Beng Jian(Bow stance and tilt sword) ………………………………………… (44)
3.15　Xie Bu Ya Jian(Rest stance and press sword) … (45)
3.16　Jin Bu Jiao Jian(Advance and circle with sword) ……………………………………… (48)
3.17　Ti Xi Shang Ci(Lift knee and thrust sword) …… (50)
3.18　Xu Bu Xia Jie(Empty stance to intercept with sword) ……………………………………… (52)
3.19　You Zuo Ping Dai(Withdraw sword to both sides) ………………………………………… (54)
3.20　Gong Bu Pi Jian(Bow stance and chop sword) ………………………………………… (56)
3.21　Ding Bu Tuo Jian(T-stance and hold sword) ………………………………………… (58)
3.22　Fen Jiao Hou Dian(Toes kick and point back) ………………………………………… (60)

3.23 Pu Bu Chuan Jian(Crouch stance and thrust sword) .... (64)
3.24 Deng Jiao Jia Jian(Heel kick and block sword) .... (66)
3.25 Ti Xi Dian Jian(Lift knee and point down) ...... (68)
3.26 Pu Bu Heng Sao(Crouch stance and sweep sword) ... . (69)
3.27 You Zuo Gong Bu Xia Jie(Bow stance and intercept on both sides) .... (70)
3.28 Gong Bu Xia Ci(Bow stance and thrust sword) .... (73)
3.29 You Zuo Yun Mo(Wave sword on both sides) ... (75)
3.30 You Gong Bu Pi(Right bow stance and chop sword) .... (79)
3.31 Hou Ju Tui Jia Jian(Raise leg backward and block) .... (81)
3.32 Ding Bu Dian Jian(T - stance and point sword) .... (82)
3.33 Ma Bu Tui Jian(Horse stance and push sword) .... (83)
3.34 Du Li Shang Tuo(Stand on one leg and hold up sword) .... (84)
3.35 Jin Bu Gua Dian(Advance to parry and point) .... (86)
3.36 Xie Bu Beng Jian (Cross stance and tilt sword) .... (88)
3.37 Gong Bu Fan Ci (Bow stance and back thrust sword) .... (90)

3.38	Zhuan Shen Xia Ci (Turn body and thrust sword) ······················· (92)
3.39	Ti Xi Ti Jian (Lift knee and sword) ··············· (94)
3.40	Xing Bu Chuan Jian (Walk and pierce sword) ··· (96)
3.41	Bai Tui Jia Jian (Wave leg and block sword) ··· (98)
3.42	Gong Bu Zhi Ci (Bow stance and thrust sword) ··· (101)
3.43	Shou Shi (Closing form) ···························· (102)

Appendix 1 A Complete Chart of the Routine ····················· (105)
Appendix 2 A Guide to Learning and Practicing the Competition Routines of Tai Ji Jian ································· (117)

1.42式太极剑竞赛套路简介

A Brief Introduction to the Competition Routine of 42 Style Tai Ji Jian

1.1 套路结构特点
The Characteristics in the Structure of the Routine

1.1.1 继承性 Preservation of the tradition

42式太极剑竞赛套路,主要吸收了传统杨式、吴式、陈式等太极剑的内容,以杨式太极剑的动作为多,整个套路具有一定的继承性。

The competition routine of 42 style Tai Ji Jian was created based mainly on the traditional Yang style while synthesizing the movements from several other Tai Ji Jian styles such as Chen, Wu and Sun styles.

1.1.2 竞赛性 Suitability for competition

42式太极剑竞赛套路在继承的基础上,还有所创新,主要在动作的选取、套路的结构等方面,做了新的调整,使之成为适应竞赛的规范套路。特别近些年,在全国的武术锦标赛上,规定了太极剑的指定动作。

Although the competition routine of 42 style Tai Ji Jian was based on the different traditional routines, there are some changes such as the implementation of new movements and a readjustment in the structure of the routine to suit the competition standards. Especially in recent years, the specific movements of this routine have been regulated in the Chinese national Wu Shu competitions.

1.1.3 合理性 Rationality

42式太极剑竞赛套路在动作编排上,注意了动作的衔接与布局,考虑到动作的难易程度,做了合理的编排,整个套路分为4段,包括18种剑法、5种步型、3种平衡、3种腿法和3个发力动作。

The arrangement of 42 style Tai Ji Jian is rational with the well connections between the movements and its sequence in accordance with the degree of difficulty. The whole routine is divided into 4 segments including 18 types of the sword techniques, 5 kinds of stances, 3 ways of balance, 3 kinds of leg techniques and 3 different ways of releasing force.

1.2 技术风格特点
The Characteristics in the Technique of the Routine

42式太极剑的主要技术风格特点为:动作外形剑正势美,端庄典雅;动作气势气贯剑器,轻灵沉稳;动作衔接自然连贯,剑势缠绵;动作劲力柔中寓刚,刚发剑响;动作速度柔和缓慢,柔中有变。在练法上劲透剑器,身剑合一。

The main technical characteristics of 42 style Tai Ji Jian are as the followings: The movements of the sword are bright and beautiful, upright and elegant; the momentum is light and agile, firm and steady with the "Qi" penetrated onto the sword; the connections are smooth and natural; the force is soft with hardness and the speed is slow, tender and changeable. When practicing, make the force flow along with the sword to "merge the sword and the body into one".

2. 42式太极剑竞赛套路核心技术学练

Learning and Practicing the Key Techniques of the Competition Routine of 42 Style Tai Ji Jian

2.1 太极剑桩功练习
The Exercises of Tai Ji Jian Zhuang Gong

2.1.1 静桩 The motionless Zhuang Gong

双手持剑的桩功练习可以增强上肢以及腿部静力性力量,提高对太极剑基本技术的认识,调息练意,不可轻视。

The main purpose of doing motionless Zhuang Gong with the sword is to improve the physical strength, to increase the understanding of basic sword techniques and to enhance your breathing and awareness. Do not neglect this exercise

持剑桩(见图 2 - 1)。
Holding sword Zhuang (Fig. 2 - 1).

图 2 - 1 Fig. 2 - 1

要点:双手持剑逐渐体会剑的重量,其他要求同徒手太极拳一样。站好桩势,注意按照太极拳的技术要点逐一检查。

万事开头难,开始练习一定很累。坚持就是胜利!
Key points: Hold the sword and feel the weight of the sword.

The rest of the requirements are similar to that of Tai Ji Quan. Pay attention to the stance and check if it is in accordance to the key points for Tai Ji Quan.

It is always difficult and hard at the very beginning but if you can keep on doing it, you will succeed in the end.

2.1.2 动桩 The moving Zhuang Gong

2.1.2.1 腕花剑（见图2-2~2-7）。Wrist cutting sword (Fig. 2-2~2-7).

要点：剪腕花时松腕，放开中、无名小指，剑体贴臂两侧。此动作可以循环反复练习。

Key points: Relax your wrist and release the middle, ring and little fingers. Put the sword close to both sides of the arms. This movement can be practiced repeatedly.

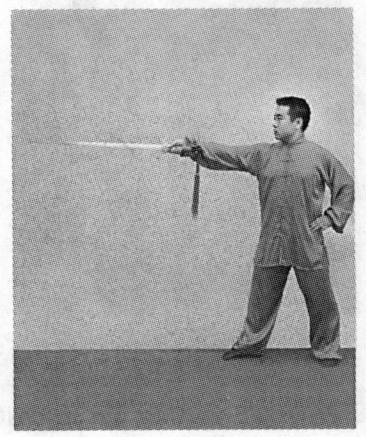

图 2-2 Fig. 2-2

图 2-3 Fig. 2-3

图2-4　Fig.2-4

图2-5　Fig.2-5

图2-6　Fig.2-6

图2-7　Fig.2-7

2.1.2.2　崩发剑(见图2-8~2-10)　Tilt sword(Fig.2-8~2-10).

要点:全身松沉,身体对拧,劲由体内逐节而发,劲透剑身。

Key points: Relax the whole body and sink down. Twist the body and make the internal force flow onto the sword.

图 2-8　Fig.2-8　　　　图 2-9　Fig.2-9

图 2-10　Fig.2-10

2.2 核心技术动作练习
The Exercises of the Key Technical Movements

2.2.1 平抹剑(见图 2 – 11 ~ 2 – 14)。 Slice with sword (Fig. 2 – 11 ~ 2 – 14).

要点:剑尖不离开身体前中线位置,用腰带动剑平行摆动。

Key points: Keep the tip of sword on the center line of the body. Use the waist to steer the movement of the sword slicing horizontally across.

图 2 – 11 Fig. 2 – 11

图 2 – 12 Fig. 2 – 12

图2-13 Fig.2-13

图2-14 Fig.2-14

2.2.2 撩剑(见图2-15～2-20)。 Cut upward with sword (Fig.2-15～2-20).

要点：身体带动剑沿体侧而出，力达剑刃。
Key points: Use the body to lead the sword out from the side of the body and move the force onto the sword blade.

2.2.3 绞剑(见图2-21～2-22) Circling sword(Fig.2-21～2-22).

要点：下肢同进步，剑、手在腰的带动下，螺旋前进。
Key points: The movements of the lower limbs are similar to that of the advancing step. Use the waist to steer the movement of the wrist and sword circling forward.

THE COMPETITION ROUTINE OF 42 STYLE TAI JI JIAN

图 2 – 15　Fig. 2 – 15

图 2 – 16　Fig. 2 – 16

图 2 – 17　Fig. 2 – 17

图 2 – 18　Fig. 2 – 18

图 2–19 Fig.2–19   图 2–20 Fig.2–20

图 2–21 Fig.2–21

图 2-22　Fig. 2-22

3.42式太极剑竞赛套路动作图解及要点

Photographs and Key Points of the Movements of the Competition Routine of 42 Style Tai Ji Jian

3.1 预备势
Yu Bei Shi(Preparing form)

图 3-1 Fig.3-1

并步持剑(见图 3-1)。Stand with feet together and hold sword (Fig.3-1).

要点:身体自然放松,敛神沉气,头颈虚领上顶,剑刃不可触及身体。

Key points: Relax your body from head to toes with concentration and inhale deeply into the abdomen. Relax your neck and keep your head straight. Don't let the sword touch the body.

第一段 Segment 1

3.2 起势
Qi Shi (Commencing form)

3.2.1 持剑开步(见图 3-2)。 Hold sword and open step (Fig. 3-2).

要点:开步时先松胯根,重心平稳过渡,防止身体侧倾。

Key points: Relax your hips when opening the step. Shift the weight steadily and don't lean the body.

3.2.2 收脚抱臂(见图 3-3 ~ 3-4)。 Withdraw foot and hold arms (Fig. 3-3 ~ 3-4).

要点:旋腰带臂,力由脚跟生。收脚、抱臂、降重心协调同步。

Key points: Twist your waist right to steer the movements of the arms with the force from the heels. Withdraw your foot, hold the arms, and lower the weight simultaneously.

图 3-2 Fig.3-2

图 3-3 Fig.3-3

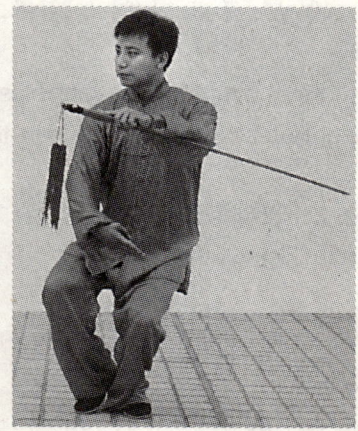

图 3-4 Fig.3-4

3.2.3 **弓步前掤**(见图 3 – 5 ~ 3 – 6)。Bow stance and ward off (Fig.3 – 5 ~ 3 – 6).

要点:右脚向右斜方上步,劲贯手臂,松肩沉肘。

Key points: Step the right foot diagonally forward to the right. Make the force flow to the arms with the shoulders relaxed and the elbows dropped.

图 3 – 5　Fig.3 – 5　　　　图 3 – 6　Fig.3 – 6

3.2.4 **跟步举指**(见图 3 – 7)。Follow up step and lift fingers (Fig.3 – 7).

要点:松右胯,重心自然平稳过渡。剑指前引与跟步配合。

Key points: Relax the right hip and shift the weight naturally. Coordinate the movements of lifting up the fingers and following up the foot.

THE COMPETITION ROUTINE OF 42 STYLE TAI JI JIAN

图 3-7   Fig.3-7

3.2.5 弓步前指(见图 3-8~3-10。)。Bow stance and point forward (Fig.3-8~3-10).

要点：右腕部自然放松竖起，指尖斜向上，手心斜向前，左手持剑需经"搂膝"动作至胯旁。

Key points: Relax the right wrist with the fingers pointing diagonally up and the palm facing forward. Hold the sword with the left hand to perform the "brush knee" movement and put the hand beside the hip.

图 3-8　Fig.3-8

图 3-9　Fig.3-9

图 3-10　Fig.3-10

3.3 并步点剑
Bing Bu Dian Jian
(Stand with feet together and point sword)

3.3.1 进步穿手(见图 3 – 11)。Advancing step and pierce hand (Fig. 3 – 11).

要点:两手的穿分要与迈步协调相合,不要分节停滞。
Key points: Coordinate the movements of piecing hands and stepping forward. Do not stop between the movements.

图 3 – 11 Fig. 3 – 11

3.3.2 收脚落剑(见图 3 – 12 ~ 3 – 13)。Withdraw foot and drop sword (Fig. 3 – 12 ~ 3 – 13).

要点:以腰带动手臂向侧分摆,手臂不要僵直。
Key points: Use your waist to steer the movement of moving the arms apart and do not straighten the arms completely.

图 3 – 12　Fig. 3 – 12　　　　图 3 – 13　Fig. 3 – 13

3.3.3 弓步交剑(见图 3 – 14 ~ 3 – 15)。Bow stance and pass sword (Fig. 3 – 14 ~ 3 – 15).

要点:左脚斜向左前方约 45 度上步,交接剑要做到准确流畅,不要停顿。
Key points: Step your foot left foward at 45 degree and pass the sword to the other hand accurately without pausing.

图 3 – 14　　Fig.3 – 14

图 3 – 15　　Fig.3 – 15

图 3 – 16　　Fig.3 – 16

3.3.4 并步点剑(见图 3 – 16)。Stand with feet together and point with sword (Fig. 3 – 16).

要点:点剑要提腕,力达剑尖。上体中正安舒,不可弓背翘臀。

Key points: Lift the wrist when pointing the sword forward with the force focused on the tip of sword. Keep the upper body upright and comfortable and do not hunch the back or stick out the buttocks.

3.4 弓步斜削
Gong Bu Xie Xiao
(Bow stance and cut obliquely)

3.4.1 撤步沉腕(见图 3 – 17 ~ 3 – 18)。Retreat and sink wrist (Fig. 3 – 17 ~ 3 – 18).

要点:以腕肘的松沉顺势带动剑尖圈绞,画一小的弧圆,提踵撤步时上体不可过度前倾。

Key points: Relax the wrist and the elbow to steer the movement of the tip of sword moving in a circular route. Do not over lean your body forward when retreating the step.

图 3 – 17　Fig. 3 – 17　　　　图 3 – 18　Fig. 3 – 18

3.4.2　转身斜削(见图 3 – 19)。Turn body and cut obliquely (Fig. 3 – 19).

要点：削剑要与转身协调一致，力达剑刃前端。
Key points: Perform the movements of cutting with the sword and turning the body simultaneously with the force focused on the tip of sword.

图 3 – 19　Fig. 3 – 19

3.5　提膝劈剑
Ti Xi Pi Jian
(Lift knee and chop sword)

3.5.1　后坐平摆(见图 3 – 20)。Sit back and wave sword (Fig. 3 – 20).

要点：后坐时松胯，使身体保持中正。
Key points: When sitting back, relax your hips to keep your body upright and centered.

图 3-20 Fig.3-20

图 3-21 Fig.3-21

3.5.2 提膝劈剑(见图 3-21~3-22)。Lift knee and chop with sword (Fig.3-21~3-22).

要点:独立起身时,头顶悬领,提膝独立与劈剑一致,保持平衡。

Key points: Relax your neck and keep your head straight when raising the body. Coordinate the movements of lifting the knee and chopping and keep your body balanced.

图 3-22　Fig.3-22

3.6　左弓步拦
Zuo Gong Bu Lan
(Left bow stance and parry sword)

3.6.1　落步圈剑(见图 3-23)。Drop foot and circle with sword (Fig.3-23).

要点:圈剑时要松腕活指,不能握死剑把。
Key points: Relax the wrist and fingers as you circle the sword. Do not hold it too tight.

3.6.2　转身拦剑(见图 3-24)。Turn body and parry with sword (Fig.3-24).

要点:拦剑手臂外旋,剑尖低于手腕,对应身体中轴。

THE COMPETITION ROUTINE OF 42 STYLE TAI JI JIAN

图 3 - 23   Fig.3 - 23   图 3 - 24   Fig.3 - 24

Key points: Turn out the left arm to parry with the sword. Put the tip of sword lower than the wrist and align the center line of your body.

3.7 左虚步撩
Zuo Xu Bu Liao
(Left empty stance and cut upward sword)

3.7.1 后坐收剑(见图 3 - 25)。Sit back and withdraw sword (Fig.3 - 25).

要点:剑走立圆,贴身,后坐时应转腰回首,目随剑视。
Key points: Keep the sword close to the body and move it in a vertical circle. Turn your waist when sitting back with the eyes following the sword.

图 3 – 25　Fig. 3 – 25

3.7.2 **虚步撩剑**(见图 3 – 26 ~ 3 – 28)。Empty stance and cut upward with sword (Fig. 3 – 26 ~ 3 – 28).

要点:撩剑要与进步一致,此动作力求连贯流畅。
Key points: Perform the movements of stepping foward and cutting upward with sword simultaneously and smoothly.

3.8　右弓步撩
You Gong Bu Liao
(**Right bow stance and cut upward with sword**)

3.8.1 **活步落剑**(见图 3 – 29)。Move step and lower sword (Fig. 3 – 29).

图 3–26　Fig. 3–26

图 3–27　Fig. 3–27

图 3–28　Fig. 3–28

图 3–29　Fig.3–29

图 3–30　Fig.3–30

图 3–31　Fig.3–31

3.8.2　右弓步撩(见图 3–30 ~ 3–31)。Bow stance and cut upward with sword (Fig.3–30 ~ 3–31).

3.9 提膝捧剑
Ti Xi Peng Jian
(Lift knee and hold sword in both hands)

3.9.1 后坐抽带(见图3-32)。Sit back and draw sword (Fig. 3-32).

要点：转腰抽剑,手有向后抽拉之劲,仿佛将剑从鞘中抽出,剑身不可随意摆动。

Key points: Turn your waist to draw the sword. There should be a pulling force as if the sword is being drawn out from its sheath and don't sway the sword.

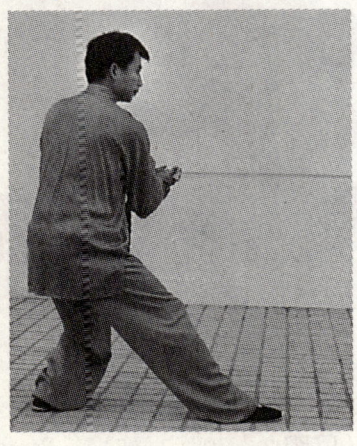

图3-32　Fig.3-32

3.9.2 **虚步分按(见图 3 – 33)。** Empty stance and press apart (Fig. 3 – 33).

要点：剑要随身体摆动，左右分带，剑尖要始终对正前方，重心后移要平稳。

Key points: Keep the sword swaying with the body with the tip of sword facing forward. Shift your weight back steadily.

图 3 – 33 Fig. 3 – 33   图 3 – 34 Fig. 3 – 34

3.9.3 **提膝捧剑(见图 3 – 34)。** Lift knee and hold sword in both hands (Fig. 3 – 34).

要点：提膝与捧剑要同起，膝肘相吸。

Key points: Perform the movements of lifting the knee and holding the sword in both hands simultaneously. Align the right elbow and the right knee.

3.10 蹬脚前刺
Deng Jiao Qian Ci
(Heel kick and thrust sword)

见图 3-35。Fig.3-35.

要点：剑与脚同出，蹬脚不得低于腰部。

Key points: Stick out the sword and your foot together. The right leg should be kept higher than your waist level.

图 3-35　Fig.3-35

3.11 跳步平刺
Tiao Bu Ping Ci
(Jump step and thrust sword)

3.11.1 提踵托刺(见图 3 – 36 ~ 3 – 37)。Lift your heel and thrust sword (Fig. 3 – 36 ~ 3 – 37).

要点：头向上领，右脚蹬地提踵，身体前探，剑前刺，有追击之意。

Key points: Lift your head up, push the right foot and lift the heel. Move your body forward and thrust the sword like chasing the opponent.

图 3 – 36　Fig. 3 – 36

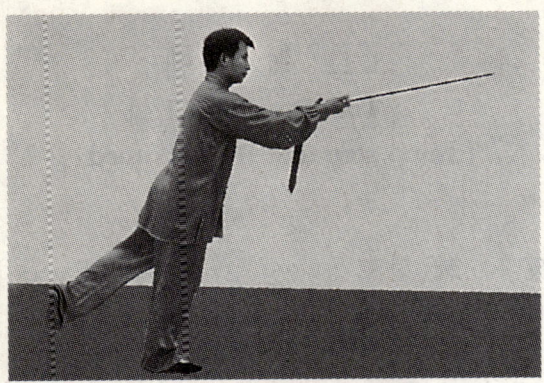

图 3－37 Fig.3－37

3.11.2 换跳落剑(见图 3－38)。Change step and lower sword (Fig.3－38).

要点：落地呼气，落步与落剑一致。
Key points: Exhale when you land. Drop the step and lower the sword at the same time.

3.11.3 弓步平刺(见图 3－39～3－40)。Bow stance and thrust sword (Fig.3－39～3－40).

要点：刺剑时顺肩前送，要有力撑八面之劲。
Key points: Move your shoulders forward when thrusting the sword with an expanding force on all sides.

图 3 – 38　Fig. 3 – 38　　　　　图 3 – 39　Fig. 3 – 39

图 3 – 40　Fig. 3 – 40

3.12 转身下刺
Zhuan Shen Xia Ci
（Turn body and thrust down）

3.12.1 后坐盘带(见图 3 – 41 ~ 3 – 42)。Sit back and draw sword back (Fig. 3 – 41 ~ 3 – 42).

要点：后坐时右胯根松缩回抽，重心平行后移。
Key points: Relax your right hip and draw the sword in as you sit back. Shift your weight back steadily.

图 3 – 41　Fig. 3 – 41

3.12.2 转身下刺(见图 3 – 43 ~ 3 – 46)。Turn body and thrust down (Fig. 3 – 43 ~ 3 – 46).

要点：右脚内扣要充分，右脚提踵，拧腰发力转体。

图 3－42　Fig.3－42

图 3－43　Fig.3－43

Key points: Turn the right foot inward, lift the right heel and twist the waist to turn your body.

图 3－44　Fig.3－44

图 3－45　Fig.3－45

图 3–46　Fig.3–46

第二段　Segment 2

3.13　弓步平斩
Gong Bu Ping Zhan
(Bow stance and cut horizontally)

3.13.1　收脚圈绞(见图 3–47)。Withdraw foot and circle sword (Fig.3–47).

要点：旋臂、沉腕，使剑尖做一顺时针方向的小弧。
Key points: Circle the arms with the wrist sunk to make the sword move in a clockwise circular direction.

图 3 – 47　Fig. 3 – 47

3.13.2　转身平斩(见图 3 – 48 ~ 3 – 49)。Turn body and cut horizontally (Fig. 3 – 48 ~ 3 – 49).

要点:以腰带臂,力注剑身。

Key points: Use the waist to steer the movement of the arm with the force focused on the sword.

图 3-48　Fig.3-48　　　　图 3-49　Fig.3-49

3.14　弓步崩剑
Gong Bu Beng Jian
(Bow stance and tilt sword)

3.14.1　插步下截(见图 3-50~3-51)。Cross step and intercept (Fig.3-50~3-51).

要点：以腰脊为轴带动剑上架，再下截。

Key points: Use the waist as the axis to block with the sword over your head and to intercept.

图 3-50　Fig.3-50　　　　图 3-51　Fig.3-51

3.14.2　弓步崩剑(见图 3-52 ~ 3-54)。Bow stance and tilt sword (Fig.3-52 ~ 3-54).

要点：拧腰蓄劲，由腰、肩、肘、腕节节贯传发力。
Key points: Twist your waist to collect the force and release it from the waist to the shoulder, the elbow and the wrist.

3.15　歇步压剑
Xie Bu Ya Jian
(Rest stance and press sword)

见图 3-55 ~ 3-56。Fig.3-55 ~ 3-56.

要点：剑身不低于脚踝，力点在剑脊。

THE COMPETITION ROUTINE OF 42 STYLE TAI JI JIAN

图 3 – 52 Fig. 3 – 52

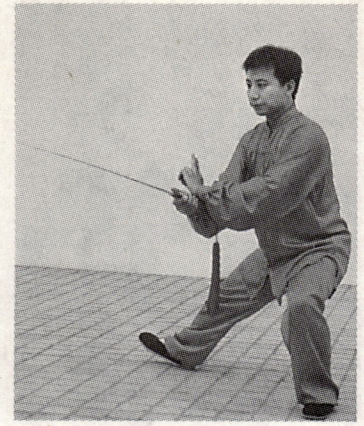

图 3 – 53 Fig. 3 – 53

图 3 – 54 Fig. 3 – 54

Key points: Press down the sword but do not lower than the ankle. Focus the force on the sword.

图 3－55　Fig.3－55　　　　图 3－56　Fig.3－56

图 3－57　Fig.3－57

3.16 进步绞剑
Jin Bu Jiao Jian
（Advance and circle with sword）

3.16.1 虚步提剑(见图3-57)。Empty stance and raise sword (Fig.3-57).

要点：手腕放松上提，剑尖要低于手腕。提剑、起身和出虚步同步完成。

Key points: Raise the sword with the wrist relaxed and keep the tip of sword lower than the wrist. Perform the movements of raising the sword and stepping out simultaneously.

图3-58　Fig.3-58

图 3-59　Fig.3-59

图 3-60　Fig.3-60

3.16.2　**上步绞剑**(见图 3-58~3-61)。Step foward and circle with sword (Fig.3-58~3-61).

要点:上步时,重心要轻灵平稳,以腰身带动剑身螺旋圈绞,一步一绞,劲力连绵不断。

图 3-61　Fig.3-61

Key points: When stepping forward, move your weight steadily and agilely. Use the waist to steer the movement of circling the sword with one step for one circle, and make the force flow continuously.

3.17　提膝上刺
Ti Xi Shang Ci
(Lift knee and thrust sword)

3.17.1　后坐带剑(见图3-62)。Sit back and withdraw sword (Fig.3-62).

要点：立身中正，松胯圆裆，转腰后坐，带动剑弧形回抽。

Key points: Keep your body upright and centered. Relax the

hip and keep your groin rounded. Turn the waist and sit back to draw the sword back in an arc route.

图 3－62 Fig.3－62

3.17.2 独立上刺(见图 3－63)。Stand on one leg and thrust up (Fig.3－63).

要点：起身时，沉裆走下弧过渡，重心至右腿。头领，立身，独立。刺剑与提膝一致。

Key points: When rising up, shift your weight to the right leg with the groin sunk. Lift your head up, keep the body upright and stand on one leg. Thrust the sword and raise the knee at the same time.

图 3 – 63 Fig. 3 – 63

3.18 虚步下截
Xu Bu Xia Jie
(Empty stance to intercept with sword)

3.18.1 落脚格带(见图 3 – 64)。Drop foot and withdraw sword (Fig. 3 – 64).

要点:先松垮,屈膝半蹲落脚,与转腰、格带剑协调相合。

Key points: Relax your hips and coordinate the movement of bending the knees and dropping the foot with turning your waist and withdrawing the sword.

图 3 – 64　Fig.3 – 64

图 3 – 65　Fig.3 – 65

3.18.2 虚步截剑(见图 3 – 65)。Empty stance and withdraw sword (Fig.3 – 65).

要点:拧腰带剑。

Key points: Twist your waist to steer the movement of the sword.

3.19 右左平带
You Zuo Ping Dai
(Withdraw sword to both sides)

3.19.1 弓步右带(见图 3-66~3-68)。Bow stance and withdraw sword to the right (Fig.3-66~3-68).

要点:带剑时,剑先向前伸,与上步一致,成弓步与后带一致,力点在剑刃。

Key points: When withdrawing the sword, extend the sword forward and at the same time step foward. Do the movements of forming the bow stance and withdrawing the sword simltaneously with the force focused on the blade of sword.

图 3-66 Fig.3-66   图 3-67 Fig.3-67

图 3 - 68　Fig.3 - 68

图 3 - 69　Fig.3 - 69

图 3 - 70　Fig.3 - 70

3.19.2　弓步左带(见图 3 - 69 ~ 3 - 72)。Bow stance and withdraw sword to the left (Fig.3 - 69 ~ 3 - 72).

图 3-71　Fig.3-71　　　　图 3-72　Fig.3-72

3.20　弓步劈剑
Gong Bu Pi Jian
(Bow stance and chop sword)

3.20.1　盖步下截(见图 3-73)。Cross step and withdraw sword(Fig.3-73).

要点：转腰幅度要大一些，身体略前倾。下截利用拧腰之劲。

Key points: Turn your waist and lean your body forward slightly. Use the force generated from twisting the waist to intercept.

图 3-73　Fig.3-73

图 3-74　Fig.3-74

3.20.2　弓步抡劈(见图3-74~3-75)。Bow stance to swing and chop (Fig.3-74~3-75).

要点:力由背发,通过肩、肘到手,力贯剑身,臂与剑成一直线。

Key points: The force comes from the back and flows

through the shoulders to the elbows and reaches your hands and the sword. Keep the arm and the sword in a straight line.

图 3-75 Fig. 3-75

3.21 丁步托剑
Ding Bu Tuo Jian
（T - stance and hold sword）

3.21.1 提膝下截(见图 3-76)。Lift knee and intercept(Fig. 3-76).

要点：支撑腿为屈膝半蹲，提膝与下截同步。
Key points: The supporting leg is half bended. Lift your knee and intercept at the same time.

3.21.2 丁步上托(见图 3-77～3-78)。T - stance and hold sword up (Fig. 3-77～3-78).

要点：上托时保持剑身横平，劲贯剑身上刃。

图 3-76 Fig.3-76

图 3-77 Fig.3-77

图 3-78 Fig.3-78

Key points: When holding the sword up, keep the sword horizontally straight with the force focused on the blade.

3.22 分脚后点
Fen Jiao Hou Dian
(Toes kick and point back)

3.22.1 转身挂穿(见图 3 – 79 ~ 3 – 81)。Turn body and thrust sword (Fig.3 – 79 ~ 3 – 81).

要点:仆步穿剑时,剑贴腿内侧平行于地面,立身中正,不可俯身低头。

Key points: Keep the sword on the inner side of your leg and parallel to the floor when crouching and thrusting. Keep the body upright and do not lower your head.

图 3 – 79   Fig.3 – 79   图 3 – 80   Fig.3 – 80

图 3－81　Fig.3－81

图 3－82　Fig.3－82

3.22.2　弓步刺剑(见图 3－82)。Bow stance and thrust sword (Fig.3－82).

3.22.3 并步收抱(见图 3 – 83 ~ 3 – 84)。Withdraw foot and hold sword (Fig. 3 – 83 ~ 3 – 84).

要点:以腰脊为轴拧腰带臂,剑走立圆,贴身。收脚并步与收抱剑协调同步。

Key points: Using the waist as the axis, twist your waist to steer the movement of the arms and draw the sword in a vertical circle along the side of the body. Do the movements of withdrawing the foot and holding the sword simultaneously.

图 3 – 83 Fig. 3 – 83

图 3 – 84 Fig. 3 – 84

3.22.4 独立提剑(见图 3 – 85)。Stand on one leg and raise sword (Fig. 3 – 85).

要点:立身中正,头领气沉。提膝提剑与下指协调一致。

Key points: Keep the body upright and lift your head with the "Qi" sunk down. Do the movements of lifting the knee and the sword and pointing down simultaneously.

图 3 – 85　Fig. 3 – 85　　　　图 3 – 86　Fig. 3 – 86

3.22.5　分脚后点（见图 3 – 86）。Toes kick and point back (Fig. 3 – 86).

要点：点剑力达剑尖，分脚高于腰，分脚时收住右胯根。
Key points: Point back with the force focused on the tip of sword and keep the leg higher than the waist. When separating the leg, draw in the right hip.

第三段 Segment 3

3.23 仆步穿剑
Pu Bu Chuan Jian
（Crouch stance and thrust sword）

3.23.1 转身平削（见图 3-87~3-89）。Turn body and cut with sword (Fig.3-87~3-89).

要点：以腰带转，力达剑刃。

Key points: Use your waist to steer the turning of the sword with the force focused on the blade.

图 3-87 Fig.3-87

图 3-88   Fig.3-88

图 3-89   Fig.3-89

3.23.2 仆步下穿(见图 3-90~3-91)。Crouch stance and thrust sword (Fig.3-90~3-91).

 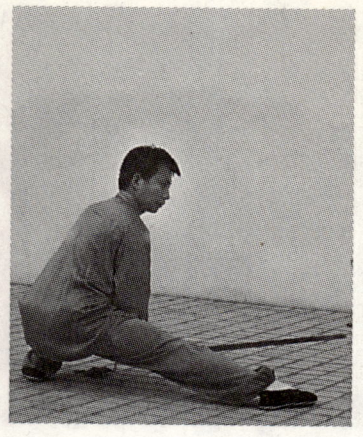

图 3-90　Fig.3-90　　　图 3-91　Fig.3-91

3.24　蹬脚架剑
Deng Jiao Jia Jian
(Heel kick and block sword)

图 3-92　Fig.3-92

图 3-93　Fig.3-93　　　　图 3-94　Fig.3-94

3.24.1　提膝上架(见图 3-92～3-94)。Lift knee and block (Fig.3-92～3-94).

3.24.2　蹬脚前指(见图 3-95)。Heel kick and point forward (Fig.3-95).

要点:蹬脚高度过腰,与前指同时伸出,蹬脚时收腹立身。

Key points: Kick with your heel over the waist level and at the same time point forward. Keep the abdomen in when kicking.

图 3–95　Fig. 3–95

3.25　提膝点剑
Ti Xi Dian Jian
（Lift knee and point down）

图 3–96　Fig. 3–96

收腿下点(见图 3-96)。Withdraw foot and point down (Fig. 3-96).

3.26 仆步横扫
Pu Bu Heng Sao
(Crouch stance and sweep sword)

仆步扫剑(见图 3-97~3-98)。Crouch stance and sweep sword (Fig. 3-97~3-98).

要点：扫剑平行贴近地面,力贯剑刃。

Key points: Sweep the sword horizontally close to the floor with the force focused on the blade.

图 3-97　Fig. 3-97

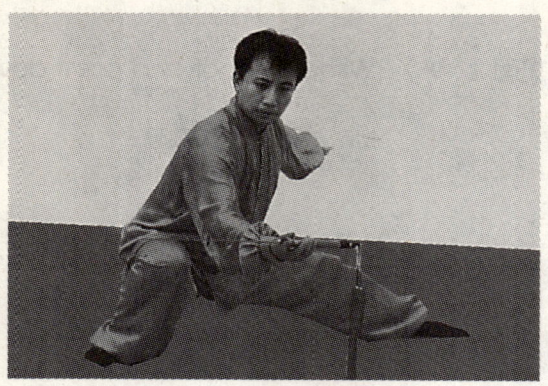

图 3-98　Fig.3-98

3.27　右左弓步下截
You Zuo Gong Bu Xia Jie
(Bow stance and intercept on both sides)

3.27.1　弓步拔剑(见图 3-99)。Bow stance and pull sword (Fig.3-99).

要点:拔剑要旋腕划弧,有拔草寻蛇之意。
Key points: Pull the sword by twisting the wrist to circle as if seeking for a snake in the grass.

3.27.2　弓步截剑(见图 3-100~3-101)。Bow stance and intercept sword (Fig.3-100~3-101).

要点:截剑与上弓步协调同出。

图 3 – 99 Fig.3 – 99

图 3 – 100 Fig.3 – 100

图 3 – 101 Fig.3 – 101

Key points: Do the movements of intercepting and forward bow stance simultaneously.

3.27.3 上步拔剑(见图3-102)。Step foward and pull sword (Fig.3-102).

要点:同右势,惟方向相反。
Key points: Similar to the movements of the right side, but in the opposite direction.

图3-102 Fig.3-102

3.27.4 弓步截剑(见图3-103)。Bow stance and intercept sword (Fig.3-103).

要点:同右势,惟方向相反。
Key points: Similar to the movements of the right side, but in the opposite direction.

图 3 – 103　Fig.3 – 103

3.28　弓步下刺
Gong Bu Xia Ci
（**Bow stance and thrust sword**）

3.28.1　震脚收剑(见图 3 – 104)。Stamp foot and draw sword (Fig.3 – 104).

要点：全身松沉，震脚发力。用腰转带动右臂回收右腰侧，蓄力待发。

Key points: Relax the whole body and sink down to stamp your foot. Turn your waist to draw the sword back at the right side of the waist to collect the force.

THE COMPETITION ROUTINE OF 42 STYLE TAI JI JIAN

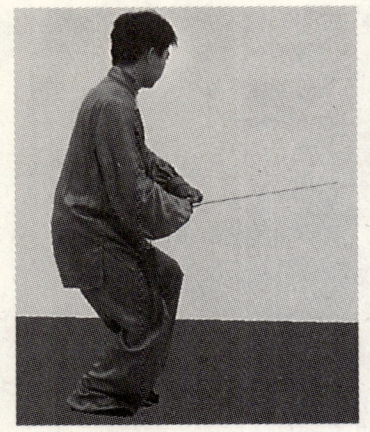

图3－104　Fig.3－104　　　　图3－105　Fig.3－105

图3－106　Fig.3－106

3.28.2　弓步下刺(见图3－105～3－106)。Bow stance and thrust sword (Fig.3－105～3－106).

要点：通过脚蹬地，拧腰节节催动将剑穿出。

Key points: Push the foot against the floor and twist your waist to thrust out the sword.

3.29 右左云抹
You Zuo Yun Mo
(Wave sword on both sides)

3.29.1 盖步云剑(右势)(见图 3 - 107 ~ 109)。Front cross stance and wave sword (right) (Fig. 3 - 107 ~ 109).

要点:盖步时,提踵以前脚掌先着地,步法力求轻灵飘逸。云剑时,以腰带剑,在头顶上螺旋盘绕,头略上仰,使剑在头顶高度,面前云过,力在剑身。

Key points: When doing the front cross stance, drop the sole lightly onto the floor and try to make the footwork as agile as possible. When waving the sword, use your waist to steer the movement of circling the sword above your head and look up slightly with the force focused on the blade.

3.29.2 弓步抹剑(见图 3 - 110 ~ 3 - 111)。Bow stance and slice sword (Fig. 3 - 110 ~ 3 - 111).

要点:抹剑力在剑刃,此势与云剑一气呵成,不可断劲停顿。

Key points: Focus the force on the blade and complete this movement continuously with the previous one without any intervals in between.

图 3 – 107 Fig. 3 – 107

图 3 – 108 Fig. 3 – 108

图 3 – 109 Fig. 3 – 109

图 3-110　Fig.3-110　　　图 3-111　Fig.3-111

3.29.3　盖步云剑(左势)(见图 3-112～3-113)。Front cross stance and wave sword (left) (Fig.3-112～3-113).

要点：同右势盖步云剑,惟方向相反。
Key points: Similar to the movements of the right side, but in the opposite direction.

3.29.4　弓步抹剑(见图 3-114～3-115)。Bow stance and slice sword (Fig.3-114～3-115).

要点：同右势弓步抹剑,惟方向相反。
Key points: Similar to the movements of the right side, but in the opposite direction.

图 3–112　Fig.3–112

图 3–113　Fig.3–113

图 3–114　Fig.3–114

图 3 – 115　Fig. 3 – 115

3.30　右弓步劈
You Gong Bu Pi
(Right bow stance and chop sword)

图 3 – 116　Fig. 3 – 116

3.30.1 收脚落剑(见图 3 – 116)。Withdraw foot and lower sword (Fig. 3 – 116).

3.30.2 弓步劈剑(见图 3 – 117)。Bow stance and chop sword (Fig. 3 – 117).

要点：用腰带臂顺肩抢劈，力贯剑身。

Key points: Use your waist to steer the movement of the arms and extend your shoulders to swing chop with the force focused on the blade.

图 3 – 117   Fig. 3 – 117

3.31 后举腿架剑
Hou Ju Tui Jia Jian
(Raise leg backward and block)

3.31.1 盖步挂剑(见图 3 – 118)。Front step and parry sword (Fig.3 – 118).

要点：剑走立圆贴身。
Key points：Draw the sword in a vertical circle along the side of the body.

图 3 – 118　Fig.3 – 118

图 3 – 119　Fig.3 – 119

3.31.2 举腿架剑(见图 3 – 119)。Raise leg and block sword (Fig.3 – 119).

要点:右腿后举与举剑上架一致,身体拧转,保持平衡。

Key points: Do the movements of raising the right leg backward and blocking with the sword simultaneously. Twist your body and keep the balance.

3.32 丁步点剑
Ding Bu Dian Jian
（T – stance and point sword）

图 3 – 120　Fig.3 – 120

图 3 – 121　Fig.3 – 121

见图 3 – 120 ~ 3 – 121。Fig. 3 – 120 ~ 3 – 121.

3.33 马步推剑
Ma Bu Tui Jian
(Horse stance and push sword)

3.33.1 撤步收剑(见图 3 – 122)。Retreat step and draw sword (Fig. 3 – 122).

要点：抽收右腰根，蓄劲待发。
Key points: Draw your right hip in and collect the force.

图 3 – 122　Fig. 3 – 122　　　图 3 – 123　Fig. 3 – 123

3.33.2 马步推剑(见图 3-123)。Horse stance and push sword (Fig.3-123).

要点:转腰沉胯,马步侧出发力。力贯剑身。

Key points: Turn your waist with the hips sunk. Push the waist forward with the force focused on the sword.

第四段 Segment 4

3.34 独立上托
Du Li Shang Tuo
(Stand on one leg and hold up sword)

3.34.1 插步绕剑(见图 3-124)。Back cross step and circle sword (Fig.3-124).

要点:剑贴身立圆下挂,与插步协调一致。

Key points: Draw the sword in a vertical circle along the side of the body to parry while stepping back.

3.34.2 蹲转扫剑(见图 3-125)。Squat, turn and sweep sword (Fig.3-125).

要点:以左脚跟、右脚掌为轴辗转,做到平稳连贯。

Key point: Use the left heel and the right sole as the pivots to turn.

图 3－124　　Fig.3－124

图 3－125　　Fig.3－125

图 3－126　　Fig.3－126

图 3－127　　Fig.3－127

3.34.3 独立上托(见图 3 – 126 ~ 3 – 127)。Stand on one leg and hold up sword (Fig. 3 – 126 ~ 3 – 127).

3.35 进步挂点
Jin Bu Gua Dian
(Advance to parry and point)

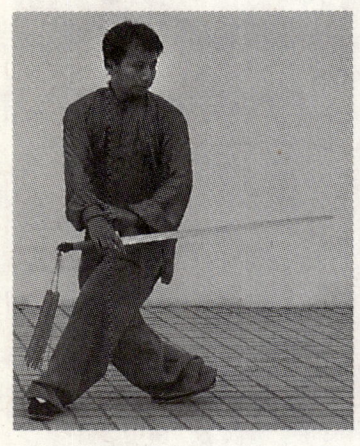 

图 3 – 128　Fig. 3 – 128　　图 3 – 129　Fig. 3 – 129

3.35.1 上步挂剑(见图 3 – 128 ~ 3 – 129)。Step foward and parry sword (Fig. 3 – 128 ~ 3 – 129).

要点：挂剑时转腰、转胯、扣腕，剑尖前领，贴身，立圆。
Key points: Turn your waist and hip when parrying. Bend the wrist and point the tip of sword forward in a vertical circle.

图 3 – 130   Fig. 3 – 130

图 3 – 131   Fig. 3 – 131

3.35.2 **虚步点剑**(见图 3 – 130 ~ 3 – 132)。Empty stance and point sword (Fig. 3 – 130 ~ 3 – 132).

图 3-132   Fig.3-132

3.36 歇步崩剑
Xie Bu Beng Jian
(Cross stance and tilt sword)

3.36.1 弓步反撩(见图 3-133~3-134)。Bow stance and cut upward (Fig.3-133~3-134).

要点:反撩时,反手持剑,旋臂扣肩,力在剑刃。

Key points: While cutting, twist the arm and lower the shoulder with the force focused on the blade.

3.36.2 歇步崩剑(见图 3-135~3-136)。Cross stance and tilt sword (Fig.3-135~3-136).

要点:立身下坐,手腕松沉。

图 3 – 133　Fig.3 – 133

图 3 – 134　Fig.3 – 134

Key points: Keep your body upright and sink down with the wrist relaxed.

THE COMPETITION ROUTINE OF 42 STYLE TAI JI JIAN

图 3-135 Fig.3-135   图 3-136 Fig.3-136

3.37 弓步反刺
Gong Bu Fan Ci
(Bow stance and back thrust sword)

见图 3-137~3-139。Fig.3-137~3-139.

要点:劲起于右脚蹬地,由下向上通于背,旋臂刺剑,力达剑尖。

Key points: Collect the force by pushing the right foot against the floor and let it flow through the back into the arms to thrust the sword out and make the force reach the tip of sword.

图 3 – 137   Fig.3 – 137   图 3 – 138   Fig.3 – 138

图 3 – 139   Fig.3 – 139

3.38 转身下刺
Zhuan Shen Xia Ci
(Turn body and thrust sword)

3.38.1 马步扣剑(见图 3 - 140)。Horse stance and point back (Fig.3 - 140).

要点:左脚内扣与扣腕反点一致。
Key points: Turn the left foot inward while pointing back.

图 3 - 140 Fig.3 - 140   图 3 - 141 Fig.3 - 141

3.38.2 弓步下刺(见图 3 - 141 ~ 3 - 144)。Bow stance and thrust sword (Fig.3 - 141 ~ 3 - 144).

要点:以左脚掌为轴,脚跟不可高提。

Key points: Perform this movement using the left sole as the axis and do not raise the heels.

图 3 – 142　Fig.3 – 142

图 3 – 143　Fig.3 – 143

图 3－144 Fig.3－144

3.39 提膝提剑
Ti Xi Ti Jian
（Lift knee and sword）

3.39.1 转腰带剑(见图 3－145)。Turn waist and withdraw sword (Fig.3－145).

要点：旋腰带臂，摆剑。

Key points: Twist your waist to steer the movement of the arms and swing the sword.

3.39.2 提膝提剑(见图 3－146～3－147)。Lift knee and sword (Fig.3－146～3－147).

要点：提膝与提剑一致。

Key points: Lift the knee and the sword simultaneously.

图 3 – 145　Fig.3 – 145　　　　　图 3 – 146　Fig.3 – 146

图 3 – 147　Fig.3 – 147

3.40 行步穿剑
Xing Bu Chuan Jian
(Walk and pierce sword)

见图 3－148～3－153。Fig. 3－148～3－153.

要点：行步时，抽住两胯根，保持行走平稳，速度均匀。走时意想剑尖追击身后之敌。

Key points: When walking, draw in both hips in order to move steadily and consistently and imagine that you are using the tip of sword chasing after the enemy behind you.

图 3－148   Fig. 3－148

图 3 – 149   Fig.3 – 149

图 3 – 150   Fig.3 – 150

图 3 – 151   Fig.3 – 151

图 3－152　Fig.3－152　　　图 3－153　Fig.3－153

3.41　摆腿架剑
Bai Tui Jia Jian
（Wave leg and block sword）

3.41.1　云剑摆腿（见图 3－154～3－155）。Wave sword and leg (Fig.3－154～3－155).

要点：用腰带动腿和剑摆动。

Key points: Use your waist to steer the movements of waving the sword and the foot.

图 3 – 154　　Fig.3 – 154

图 3 – 155　　Fig.3 – 155

图 3 – 156　　Fig.3 – 156

3.41.2 落步平抹(见图3-156)。Drop step and slice sword (Fig.3-156).

要点:落步时,先屈膝松髋。
Key points: When dropping the step, bend the left knee and relax your hips.

图3-157　Fig.3-157

3.41.3 弓步架剑(见图3-157)。Bow stance and block sword (Fig.3-157).

3.42 弓步直刺
Gong Bu Zhi Ci
(Bow stance and thrust sword)

图 3 – 158   Fig.3 – 158

3.42.1 收脚落剑(见图 3 – 158)。Withdraw foot and lower sword (Fig.3 – 158).

3.42.2 弓步前刺(见图 3 – 159 ~ 3 – 160)。Bow stance and thrust sword (Fig.3 – 159 ~ 3 – 160).

要点:蹬地前刺,力透剑尖。

Key points: Push the right foot forward with the force focused on the tip of sword.

图 3 – 159　Fig. 3 – 159　　　图 3 – 160　Fig. 3 – 160

3.43 收势
Shou Shi
（Closing form）

见图 3 – 161 ~ 3 – 165。Fig. 3 – 161 ~ 3 – 165.

要点：气沉丹田，周身放松，按指立身，气定神敛。

Key points: Breathe naturally and deeply with the "Qi" sunk to "Dan Tian". Relax your body from head to toes and press down the fingers. Keep your body upright and calm down.

图 3－161　Fig.3－161

图 3－162　Fig.3－162

图 3－163　Fig.3－163

图 3－164　Fig.3－164

图 3 – 165   Fig. 3 – 165

附 录 1　　整个套路动作路线图
Appendix 1　A Complete Chart of the Routine

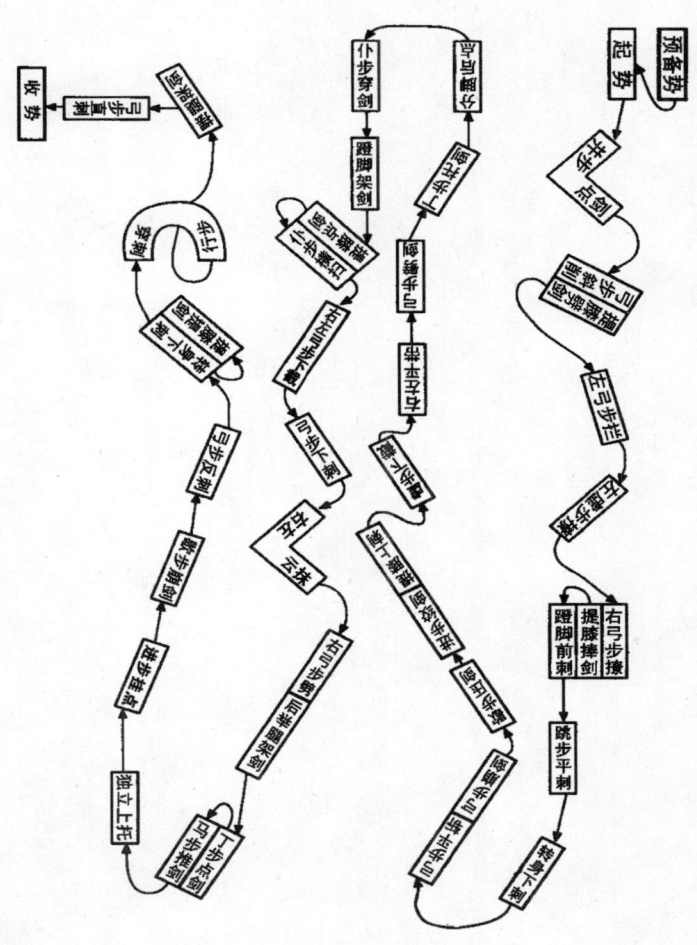

附录2　　学练太极拳竞赛套路指南

太极拳竞赛套路只是用来竞赛的吗

太极拳竞赛套路虽然名为"竞赛"套路,其实,它的功能绝对不仅仅限于竞赛,它具有明显的健身效果,这是因为竞赛套路具有如下特性:

1. 科学性

太极拳竞赛套路注重运用人体运动规律,符合人体生理特点,能促进身心健康,比如竞赛套路的编排一般是由易到难,运动量由小到大,逐渐趋于平缓。

2. 全面性

太极拳竞赛套路非常注意左右肢的均衡发展,动作对称分布,而且技术内容丰富,非常利于人体全面锻炼,促进身心健康。

3. 适应性

各式太极拳竞赛套路,能满足不同人的需求,为了健身的需要,竞赛套路完全可以根据具体情况而变化,具有良好的适应性,比如老年人学练时,完全可以不做难度大的动作,去掉或降低一定的动作数量及要求,还可因自身条件而决定做哪些动作。据北京体育大学对各式太极拳竞赛套路的科学研究证实,长期坚持学练太极拳竞赛套路,能够恢复和增强神经、血液循环、消化等各大系统的功能,具有良好的健身作用。

如何选练太极拳竞赛套路

1.因人因式

每个人的身体情况、性格爱好、生理特点不同,选练太极拳竞赛套路时首先应该考虑到自身的这些条件,然后,根据各式太极拳竞赛套路的特点,选择适合自己的一式入手学练。比如身体健壮、喜欢发力的中青年人,选择陈式太极拳竞赛套路为好;年龄偏大、体质较弱的人,选择步高架活的孙式太极拳竞赛套路为宜;性格温和、喜欢安静的人,选择杨式太极拳竞赛套路较适合。总之,选择适合自己的套路学练,往往能事半功倍,收到良好的健身、竞赛效果。

2.因势因果

为了竞赛而学练太极拳竞赛套路时,除了考虑自身特点外,还应根据各式太极拳竞赛的形势和预期结果而选项,比如全国、国际的太极拳竞赛中,男女42式太极拳、太极剑参赛人数多、水平高,男子陈式太极拳水平较高,女子杨式太极拳竞争较激烈,而男子孙式太极拳、女子陈式太极拳以及男女武式太极拳、吴式太极拳参赛人数较少,竞争相对弱些,对于一般选手而言,应选取相对容易取得名次的项目作为突破口。

如何学好太极拳竞赛套路

1.满怀信心,明确目标

学好太极拳竞赛套路,首先应该满怀信心,明确目标。如果是为了健身,就一定要坚信,学练太极拳能促进身心健康。如果是为了竞赛,就要有必胜的信心,不怕困难与挫折,不断进取,不懈努力,相信功夫不负有心人。

2. 读书看盘，投师访友

随着信息技术的飞速发展，学练者可以通过文字、声像及多媒体的教材，认真读书钻研，观摩示范，是学好太极拳竞赛套路的重要手段之一，甚至能无师自通。实践证明，有相当一部分人是通过这种渠道的学练，不仅练好了身体，而且，还在竞赛中取得了好成绩。当然，在自己看光盘、读书学习的基础上，有条件的尽可能请名师指导，口传身授，会有意想不到的收获。

3. 循序渐进，精益求精

初学太极拳竞赛套路，应该循序渐进，不可贪多求快。应本着精益求精的思想，反复学习每一个动作，包括定型动作、要点、方位轨迹等都要清清楚楚，以免养成错误的动作习惯，影响整个技术的提高，以及健身竞赛效果。自学的方法最好是动静结合，所谓动是要跟着光盘学练，动起来；所谓静是要认真看书中的图解，仔细琢磨，一个动作一个动作的推敲学习，切记不要囫囵吞枣，贪多求快。

如何练好太极拳竞赛套路

1. 打好基础，勤练不辍

基础练习包括太极拳的基本身心素质、基本动作等内容，要练好太极拳竞赛套路，这是基石，否则难以构筑技术高峰。必须打好扎实的基础，对必要的柔韧素质、平衡能力、基本动作要进行严格、艰苦和勤奋练习，即使达到了一定水平，也不能放松，绝不能丢弃基础性练习，这是成功的保证。如本系列丛书提供的各式太极拳和太极剑的静桩、动桩，就是十分有效的基础练习内容，需要贯彻始终，勤练不辍。

2. 抓住核心，意形兼练

太极拳竞赛套路都有明确的技术要求，本系列丛书介绍了各式太极拳的核心技术，抓住这些技术进行学练，会事半功倍地提高你的水平。在看书的同时,还要注意观看光盘的示范,体会太极拳的意气神韵,突出太极拳运动的特点,这也是练好太极拳竞赛套路的关键,防止练拳时不讲意识引导动作,失去劲力内涵,演化成太极操。

如何参加太极拳竞赛套路的竞赛

1. 遵守规则,注意细节

由于太极拳竞赛套路有明确统一的动作规则,竞赛中裁判员一般都依据规则来评判,所以要尽可能按照规则要求做动作,避免所做动作与套路规则内容不符,出现动作方向、数量与规则不同的错误,以至造成不必要的扣分。这里需要特别注意,有时看书学套路不容易学到位,比如,陈式太极拳竞赛套路早期的版本中,起势动作中有划圈的描写,但是,幅度不大,而我们在实际的教学中划的是大圈,这些细节应仔细看光盘学习。还有一点要特别注意,就是每次竞赛时规程的要求以及大会对动作规则的补充通知,比如同样的套路动作,由于裁判长以及裁判员对动作规则理解的差异,或者是由于对套路个别地方的修改,会造成每次竞赛有细微的差别,这也会造成不必要的扣分。如42式太极剑在脚跟、脚尖落地,摆扣等问题上就有所差异,这些在竞赛前最好能取得裁判的统一认识。

2. 提高素质,避免紧张

竞赛时几乎每个人或多或少都有些紧张,赛场上常常可以看到运动员手脚发抖、失去平衡、动作变形的现象,这些很大程度是由心理因素造成的。据统计,遥测全国太极拳竞赛场上运动员心率,有的高达180次/分。本不属于大强度运动的太极拳,为什么有如此高的心率反应呢?主要还是紧张造成的,按太极拳的技术要求应该是"心静体松"。但是,由于竞赛很难让运动员心理真正放松,所以,首先要让运动员正确认识和对待紧张。紧张是一种正常的生理、心理现象,几乎是每个人都有,只是程度不同而已,不必恐惧焦虑。其次,有意增加模拟性竞赛练习,提高心理素质。第三,出现极度紧张,往往是在分脚独立时产生,所以要加强相关动作所需身体素质的练习。最后,不妨从学练太极拳竞赛套路中找原因,看看自己是否按太极拳运动要领学练的,虚领顶劲,以意导体,气沉丹田,排除杂念。总之,逐渐通过综合性学练提高心理素质、身体素质、技术水平,减小紧张程度。

3. 做好准备,适时上场

竞赛前合理有效的准备活动能明显提高竞赛成绩。这里应包括对场地地质、演练方向、准备活动时间等方面的了解。一般来讲,距上场前20～30分钟做准备活动较好,轻微慢跑、比划套路、重点动作练习等均为主要准备活动内容,以身体微微出汗、周身舒服为度,脉搏控制在120次/分以下较为适宜。当然,每个人的习惯不同,不必强求,以能活动开、发挥最好技术水平为准。另外,还要注意到赛场的场地情况,有无地毯、地毯的质地如何、上场时是几个人、站位情况、演练的方向要求、所穿鞋的厚薄质地等,这些小问题,也必须重视,否则会因小失大。

各式太极拳竞赛套路的风格特点是什么,学练中怎样注意相关的技术差异

各式太极拳竞赛套路有着很多共性的地方,比如都要求用意识引导动作,刚柔相济,相对缓慢等;动作名称、套路结构相似等。但是,各式太极拳竞赛套路又有着各自不同的特点,具体的技术差异表现为:

1. 陈式太极拳竞赛套路

陈式太极拳竞赛套路节奏鲜明,气势宏大。练习中,要突出缠丝劲法及松活弹抖的发力,表现出陈式太极拳竞赛套路独特的风格特点。具体表现在以躯干的缠绕为主,通过腰脊的螺旋转动和胸腹的折叠变化来贯串上肢和下肢的螺旋缠丝,达到周身缠丝。外形上,上肢两臂旋腕转膀,形如拧麻花状;下肢两腿旋踝转腿,似拧钻螺丝之形。发力上,防止过分追求发力效果,以至于发僵直劲,或发虚假劲。发力后尤其注意与下边动作的自然衔接,避免断劲。

解决方法:要发好力,应由"极柔软"再至"极坚刚"。开始时多注意由内动引导肢体的放长、螺旋缠绕,逐渐发力,还应专门进行单势发力练习及其他辅助练习如柔韧性练习,抖大杆子等。

陈式太极拳竞赛套路手型也很特殊,不同于其他式太极拳竞赛套路的手型,主要表现为掌型为瓦楞形的螺旋状,大拇指根合向小指,指尖后仰,这与陈式特点及技击作用有关,练习时应注意,防止陈式、杨式掌型混同。陈式的勾型是五指尖自然捏拢也不同于其他式,应引起大家注意。擦脚出步是陈式的步法特点。往往有擦不着脚的问题,除了与地质有关外,主要是与虚实、腿力大小有关。另外,还应正确掌握擦脚的距离。平时要专门练习步法,加强腿力练习(以桩功为主)。

2.杨式太极拳竞赛套路

杨式太极拳竞赛套路重点突出动作外形的舒展大方,动作过程的柔和缓慢。整个套路具有连贯圆活、沉稳舒展、形象优美的独特风格。防止过分追求动作柔、姿势低、幅度大、造型美,造成动作变形,出现跪膝、拔跟毛病;动作轻飘,出现柔软操化、失去轻灵中的沉稳,没有内劲。

解决方法:在规定动作基础上,强调太极拳技术要求,适当的辅以功法、推手练习,来帮助学练者正确理解太极拳运动本质特点,保持项目自身的特色。

3.武式太极拳竞赛套路

武式太极拳竞赛套路有自己突出的特色,每个动作的过程都有"起、承、开、合"的要求。从动作外形看,在一个个节序之间似有稍顿的现象,但是,实际上动作意识并没有断,只是在贯劲,追求内动、内劲,而且每个动作都有这4个过程,有时是几个完整拳势被列入一个节序,但同样要有起承开合过程,这是一个重要特色。

防止练习时每个动作节序不清,动作不到位,一滑而过,失去武式风格。练习时,首先要从动作外形上,区别开4个过程,可以分开练,然后逐渐再连贯。

两手不出足尖也是武式太极拳竞赛套路独特的特点之一。武式太极拳竞赛套路有严格的要求,要求出手对应前脚尖,不能超出,所谓手不出足尖。很多习惯了其他式太极拳竞赛套路的人开始不容易做到这一要求。

解决方法:首先在思想认识上,明确武式太极拳竞赛套路的特点,然后再从技术上找方法,其主要方法是从关节角度上找及通过体表的标志训练慢慢养成习惯。

左右手不相逾越的要求,也是其他式太极拳竞赛套路爱好者和初学者不容易做到的技术,关键在腰的带动上,这应从身法上去练习,适当时可以用标志物限定手的轨迹。如用衣服的拉链位置,胸部的心口窝处等做参照物,限定两手的运动轨迹。

武式太极拳竞赛套路的身法特点也十分突出,要点有:含胸、拔背、裹裆、护腕、提顶、吊裆、松肩、沉肘、腾挪、闪战、尾闾正中、气沉丹田、虚实分清,这些在具体动作中,要认真体会。

4.吴式太极拳竞赛套路

吴式太极拳竞赛套路具有鲜明的技术特色,主要表现在身型上,"斜中寓正",即讲究弓腿、重心偏向前腿,如搂膝拗步、倒卷肱、上步揽雀尾、斜飞势等,看上去上体稍向前倾,而实际上头前脚后,从头顶(百会)到后脚跟,中间通过裆部,形成三点连成一条斜向地面的直线,即所谓"斜中寓正"。

步型上,突出"川"字步型,即两脚掌近似平行,脚尖、脚跟都向前;弓步步型要求前弓腿的膝与脚尖上下相对,弓步的两脚如同踏在"川"字两端上;虚步步型,要求也像"川"字一样,即虚脚点在"川"字的中竖上。还有一个特点是吴式太极拳竞赛套路中有马步,也叫桩步,其他各式太极拳竞赛套路没有明显定势的马步。手型上强调虎口张圆,拇指上竖。

学练中,注意防止为了追求"斜中寓正"而斜中不正,出现俯身、折腰、撅臀的毛病;弓步时前膝超出脚尖、后脚跟拔起、两脚之间不平行等毛病。

解决方法:首先正确理解吴式太极拳竞赛套路的风格特点,然后,增加典型动作的单势练习,适当时候可以采用客观标志物限定的方法练习。如吴式太极拳的进步练习,可以在地上做两条与肩同宽的标志线,两脚踩在线上练习,同时,辅以踝关节的柔韧练习,如压踝、揉踝等。

5.孙式太极拳竞赛套路

孙式太极拳竞赛套路的步法讲究进退相随,进步必跟、退步必撤,这是其主要技术特征之一,要求"迈步如槐虫蠕动,往来似水漂落叶",体现出步活、步点准确、步幅适中、步态轻灵的特色。迈步时,两脚始终在虚实转换当中平稳过渡,常常在裆下沉中,重心转换,而且要求身体平稳移动,没有明显的起伏。后脚跟步时,与前脚相距10厘米左右,要暗含蹬劲。退步时,松腰、沉胯反向回收脚,一进一退像是在一个浅弧形上滑动,沉稳匀速。

练习时,常出现跟步时被动提后脚,重心平移,没有内劲变化以及跟步的步点不准,距离前脚跟太近或过远,扣脚时踩脚,步态轻浮没有沉劲等毛病。

解决方法:首先,认识到步法特点的实质,然后,采用标志物(如划线)限定步幅、步点等方法,专门练习进退步法。

手法上的开合又是孙式太极拳竞赛套路的另一个重要特点。做开合手时要注意胸部气息的变化,保持坠肘、沉肩的状态。防止张肘式的开合,没有气感内劲。

解决方法:可以用阻力、助力的外力刺激,正确体会动作要点,如两掌心顶一根与脸同宽的尺子或木棍,站开手桩,解决开手两掌外翻掌心不相对的毛病。

6.42式太极拳竞赛套路

42式太极拳竞赛套路是以竞赛为主要目的、突出了规范性,包括动作外形、方位、路线等,在学练中这方面要按规则严格细抠。由于竞赛套路中兼有各式太极拳动作,往往令人不知如何做这些动作,其实,按规则及编创主旨,42式太极拳竞赛套路的风格特点与以往48式太极拳相同,基本上以杨式太极拳风格为主,对于其他式的动作这里也按"杨式"处理,但是仍要保留原动作的基本造型及基本特点,如"掩手肱捶"还要发力,但与陈式中的发力在动作的手型、步型上有所变化。再如"玉女穿梭"虽然吸收吴式的平云手法,但是身型上以中正为主,不做吴式的"斜中寓正"等等,这些应该引起注意。

7.42式太极剑竞赛套路

42式太极剑竞赛套路是目前与42式太极拳配套的惟一的一项太极拳器械竞赛套路,有的竞赛将拳和剑的成绩累加取全能名次。42式太极剑竞赛套路,主要吸收了传统杨式、吴式、陈式等太极剑的内容,以杨式太极剑的动作为主,整个套路的风格特点与42式太极拳一致,主要技术风格特点为:剑正势美、气贯剑器、轻灵沉稳、剑势缠绵、柔中寓刚、刚发剑响。

练习中最大的问题是,身与剑不合一,剑法不清楚。

解决方法:①先拳后剑,打好基础。练好太极拳是学练太极剑的基础。在太极剑中用到的身型、身法、步型、步法以及眼法,都与太极拳相一致,通过徒手拳术练习,掌握虚领顶劲、含胸拔背、连贯圆活、弧形运动等有关太极拳要求,进而练习太极剑术。②循序渐进,力求准确。初学太极剑,一招一势要力求准确。手、步、身、眼和剑法都要概念清楚,符合规范,切不可贪多求速,不求甚解,以免形成错误定型,造成"学拳容易改拳难"的局面。③先形后意,形意统一。太极剑是以意气主导的剑术,但在刚开始练剑时,还应该先重视动作外形(主要是剑法的规格),比如劈剑与点剑的区别、撩剑的运行路线等。正确的外形是用意的必备条件,当然形与意不可分,正确的用意又能促进正确外形的形成,这只是剑术练习的不同阶段侧重点不同而已,最终还是要用意导剑,形意统一,进而达到"神明"境界,动作高度自动化,形、意、神、剑合一。

Appendix 2

A Guide to Learning and Practicing the Competition Routines of Tai Ji Quan

Is the Competition Routine Only Used for Competition

Although the competition routine of Tai Ji Quan is branded as the "competition style", its function is not restricted to the competition only. It has the obvious affections on keeping fit because of the following characteristics the competition style has.

1. **Scientifically designed**

The competition routine emphasizes the biomechanical principles that are in accordance to the physiological structure of the body. This helps improve both mental and physical health. For example, the format of the competition routines is arranged in sequence according to its difficulty —— from the easy to the difficult ones, and the strength needed in the routine —— from the weak to the strong.

2. **Overall completeness**

The competition routine of Tai Ji Quan pays close attention to the balance development between the right and left parts of the body including a symmetrical layout of the movements. Besides, it is rich in its technical contents thus providing a beneficial overall workout for your health.

3. Adaptability

In order to efficiently serve its health purposes, the competition routine is accustomed to change according to the specific situations due to its adaptability. For the aged people, they are not obliged to perform the difficult movements but reducing the amount of movements or lowering the demands. They can also choose to perform certain movements according to their own health conditions. According to the research done by Beijing Sport University in the different styles of Tai Ji Quan, it has been proven that the long term training in the competition routines can recover and improve the nerve system, blood circulation, digestion and other major systems of the body with good affections for health.

How to Choose the Right Competition Routine for Yourself

1. Depends on the learner and the characteristics of different styles

People have different physical conditions, preferences and health, therefore, you should take all these into considerations before choosing one of the styles. After that, pick up the style that is suitable for yourself. For example, for young people who usually have stronger physique and more energy, it is better to choose Chen style. For the elders or those with weaker physique, Sun style will be more suitable as it has less strenuous stances. For those who prefer tranquility, or those with a mild character, they will find Yang style more appealing. In conclusion, choosing the right style of Tai Ji Quan will help you to have a more enjoyable and less stressful training, and to benefit you both in your health and in your competition.

2. **Depends on the goal of the individual and the circumstances**

For those who choose to learn the competition routine of Tai Ji Quan solely for the purpose of competing in Tai Ji Quan competitions, you should consider the trends of a certain competition style to choose besides his own physical conditions. For example, in the national and the international competitions, there are more participants in 42 style Tai Ji Quan and Tai Ji Jian both in Men's and Women's, so the competitions are fierce. For male, the competition routine of Chen style has a higher standard while for female, it's Yang style. Whereas Men's Sun style, Women's Chen style and Men's and Women's Wu style have less participants and the competition is comparatively weak. For general participants, it is wise to choose those that you may have more chance to win.

How to Learn the Competition Routines of Tai Ji Quan

1. **Be confident with definite goals**

To have a strong confidence and a focused goal are the most important factors when learning the competition routine of Tai Ji Quan. For those who learn to keep fit, they must have the faith that learning and practicing Tai Ji Quan will bring them the benefits. For those who learn for participating in the competitions, they'll have to have the strong will to win. They shouldn't be afraid of the tough training and the unavoidable setbacks, and should try to strive for every possible chance for the improvement.

2. Be well read and well informed

With the development of information technology, the learners could further enhance their knowledge and perfect their skills through reading books, listening to recorders and even using the multimedia resources, such as video tapes and VCDs. Sometimes, to the extent, that you can master the competition routines even without a coach in person. Quite a number of people are known to have learned and practiced Tai Ji Quan by using the multimedia teaching materials and some even won places in competitions besides keeping fit. But of course, if given a chance, it is always more beneficial to learn personally from masters.

3. Learn and practice systematically to perfect your skills

In the early stage of learning and practicing Tai Ji Quan, you should always try to improve your skills systematically. It is not wise to learn too much or hasten the learning pace, instead try to perfect your skills of every single movement by practicing again and again until you fully master it in case you form bad habits which will affect both your improvement of skills and scores in competitions. If you are learning Tai Ji Quan on your own (as opposed to learning from a master in person), the best way is to combine the "motion" and "motionless" aspects of Tai Ji Quan. This so called motion means to follow the video tape or VCD and practice accordingly. This so called motionless means to read the key points intensively, and pay special attention to the photographs of each movement.

How to Master the Competition Routine of Tai Ji Quan

1. **Learn the basics and practice regularly**

The basic practice includes the practice of the basic mentality and the movement etc. which are the foundation required to master the competition routine of Tai Ji Quan, otherwise, it will be really difficult to reach a high level. It is necessary to acquire the flexibility, balance and learn the basic movements through the strict, intensive and diligent training. Even after reaching a competent level, you should still need to keep on practicing the basics which can be the best guarantee to your success. For instance, the motionless and moving stances of different styles of Tai Ji Quan and Tai Ji Jian provided by this book are the best basic exercises which you need to practice regularly.

2. **Focus on the key points and have a balanced training on both the mind and the movements**

All the competition routines of Tai Ji Quan have strict technical requirements and this series provides a clear illustration of the important techniques of all the competition routines of different Tai Ji Quan styles. Mastering these important techniques will bring you a speedy and steady improvement in your skills. Apart from reading, it is also crucial to follow the demonstrations in the VCD which comes together with the books in order to understand the important aspects and features of Tai Ji Quan. It is also a good way to prevent you from performing the movements without any internal forces or meanings.

Important Hints When Taking Part in the Competitions of the Competition Routine of Tai Ji Quan

1. Obey the rules and regulations, and notice the important details

Due to the fact that there are definitive standards of performance regarding the competition routines, the referees usually judge the performance according to these standard rules. Therefore it is important for the participants to perform according to what is required in the standard and avoid the situations which would constitute violations and result in unnecessary point deductions. You should be aware that it is sometimes difficult to get the right posture when learning from books alone. For example, in the earlier version of the competition routine of Chen style, it is required to display a small circular movement at the beginning while in actual practice, what we do is a slightly bigger circular movement. That's the reason why you should refer to the videos on these differences. You should also pay special attention to the notification of changes issued before every competition which usually contains the latest amendments on the rules and the movement requirements. Sometimes the chief judge and the referees might have different interpretations regarding the movement requirements and that will some times result in slight changes in the competition process and the point deductions if you are unaware of them. For example, in the 42 style of Tai Ji Jian, there are some differences in turning foot inward and landing the heel and toes. So you should try your best to get a mutual understanding with the referees about the requirements before the competition.

2. **Improve your mentality and avoid getting too nervous during the competition**

Almost everybody gets nervous during the competition with the symptoms of the shaky limbs, losing balance or making wrong movements which are mainly caused by mental factors. Some participants may have their hearts beat as fast as 180 times per minute. Why do they have such a high heart rate while performing this less strength demanded sports? According to the studies, this is mainly due to the nervousness. We know that the technical requirement for Tai Ji Quan is "to have a peaceful mind and a relaxed body" but the competitions will definitely affect the state of your mind. Therefore the important thing is to let yourself learn to control yourself. Firstly, you need to understand that it is natural to feel nervous, so there is no need to worry about it. Secondly, you can improve your mental readiness by participating in the simulation practices. Thirdly, the extreme nervousness usually happens when performing the difficult movements like "standing on one leg". Therefore putting more effort and attention in such movements is a good way to overcome such difficulties. Lastly, it would be helpful to learn about your faults during your practice and check whether the movements are performed according to the requirements of Tai Ji Quan. In general, you can reduce your nervousness by improving the quality of your mind, your physique and

THE COMPETITION ROUTINE OF 42 STYLE TAI JI JIAN

your skills.

3. Get ready in advance and begin on time

Appropriate and sufficient preparations in advance will be helpful in getting good results during the competition. The preparations include a good knowledge of the competition ground, the direction of the performance and the duration allowed for warming up. In most cases, it is advisable to begin warming up 20 ~ 30 minutes before the competition by jogging slowly, rehearsing the full set of the routine or concentrating on the important movements. Warming up exercise is considered sufficient when you begin to perspire slightly and feel comfortable with the pulse rate around 120 times per minute. This is not, however, a universal standard for every participant since everybody has his own habits and body conditions. It is considered the best when you can best display your skills. The conditions of the competition grounds is also important. You should check whether it is carpeted, and if so, check the quality of the carpet. You should also check how many participants will be allowed to perform simultaneously and the position of yours. The direction of the performance (to the referees and judges accordingly) and the quality of the allowed costumes are also important points you need to notice.

What Are the Special Characteristics in the Competition Routines of the Different Styles of Tai Ji Quan

The competition routines of different styles of Tai Ji Quan share a lot of common characteristics such as "using your mind to

guide your movements, combining the softness and the hardness and having the similar structures and names of the movements" etc. But surely each has its own specific characteristics. The details of the differences are as the followings:

1. The competition routine of Chen style Tai Ji Quan

The competition routine of Chen style Tai Ji Quan is famous for its distinctive rhythm and the magnificent postures. When practicing, it is important to emphasize on the "spiral twisting force" and the basic requirements of relaxing, agility and springing which are the special features of Chen style Tai Ji Quan. The movements stress on the twisting of the torso. The twisting force of the upper and lower limbs are connected through the twisting motion of the spine and the changes of folding in the chest and the abdomen in order to obtain a full twisting force all over the body. For the upper limbs, twist the arm and wrist in coordinately like twisting a wet cloth dry. For the lower limbs, twist the ankles, the thighs and the calves in like driving in a screw. For the force, you should avoid over emphasize releasing the force which would result in displaying a stiff force or a false one. After releasing the force, it is imperative to maintain the continuity with the next movements without the severance in the force.

Methods to overcome such obstacles: In order to master the correct techniques of the force releasing, you should bear in mind that it is "from the extreme softness to the extreme hardness". At the beginning, you should emphasize the extension of the body movements from the internal motions to the twisting motions and finally to the external releasing of the force. It is also important to specifically train the force releasing of individual movement and other supplementary exercises such as the exercises of the flexibility and the "pole trembling" exercise.

The hand forms of Chen style Tai Ji Quan are also different from other Tai Ji Quan techniques. The main difference is that the palm is in the form of a Chinese tile and slightly retracted inward with the thumb and the little finger slightly folded and facing each other, and the tip of finger slightly pointed backward. This is in agreement with its attacking features and a distinctive difference of Chen style from others, so you should remember not to confuse it with other styles of Tai Ji Quan. The "hook form" of Chen style is also different as it is a natural clutching of all fingers. For the footwork, rubbing the moving foot with the stationary one before treading out is also a distinctive feature of Chen style. Sometimes the learners missed the rubbing motion, it is usually related to the strength in the footwork and the understanding of the "emptiness and solidity" besides the differences in the ground quality. In addition, accuracy regarding where and when the feet should rub against each other is also of great importance. You should specifically train the footwork techniques separately, and should strengthen the legs and feet through practicing standing stances.

2. **The competition routine of Yang style Tai Ji Quan**

The competition routine of Yang style emphasize the out-stretched and open-handed movements which are more gentle and slightly slower than others. The whole set has the features of the coherence, agility, outstretching with steadiness and elegance. You shculd avoid over emphasize the gentleness and the low posture or over extend the movements and paying too much attention to the visual attractiveness which would easily result in the distortion of the movements like kneeling posture and lifting heels. Over emphasize the gentleness will also result in transforming this routine into a calisthenics drill and failing to display its stability and strength.

Methods to overcome such obstacles: Focus on the key techniques of Tai Ji Quan besides practicing the standard movements. You should supplement your daily practice with the training methods such as the hand pushing exercise to understand the key and basics of Tai Ji Quan and maintain the special features of this style.

3. **The competition routine of Wu style(武式) Tai Ji Quan**

The Wu style has very prominent characteristics. Every movement strictly follows the sequence of the "commence, succession, open and close". By looking at its movement you can easily discover that although there is a consistent intermission between every major connection of movements, the momentum is not in anyway broken but carried through with the special emphasis on the internal movements and the internal strength. Sometimes a few complete movements are grouped into one combination but it still follows the sequence. This is the distinctive characteristic of Wu style.

It is important for you to avoid the ambiguous and incorrect display of the movements and the omission of the necessary sequences in case losing the color of Wu style Tai Ji Quan. When practicing, it is advisable to practice them separately by breaking the external movements into 4 sequences before connecting them up.

Another one of the characteristics of Wu style is never let

your hands extend over your feet. Wu styly has the strict requirement that the hands should be corresponded with the feet by not extending over the toes. Many practitioners who are used to practicing other competition routines are not used to this requirement.

Methods to overcome such obstacles: Understand the characteristics of Wu style Tai Ji Quan first and try to find out the ways in technique. The main method is to practice the angle of the joints, portray it onto the body postures through training and gradually form into a habit.

It is also a difficult skill for the beginners and many practitioners of other Tai Ji Quan styles in not being allowed to overlap the left and right hands. The key is the movement of the waist. You can start from training your body movements such as using signs to guide the trail of the hands. The signs can be the zip of the coat or your chest where you can refer to limit the trail of your hands.

The characteristics of the body movements in the competition routine of Wu style is very prominent. The key points are as the followings: Keep your chest in, stretch the back, round the crotch, protect the wrist, lift your head, hold the crotch, drop the shoulders and elbows, jump, deflect, align the coccyx, sink the "Qi" down to "Dan Tien", and clarify the emptiness and solidness.

4. **The competition routine of Wu style(吴式) Tai Ji Quan**

The competition routine of Wu style Tai Ji Quan has the significant characteristics mainly portrayed in its body posture "upright when slanting". It emphasizes the bow stance while having the weight leaning forward such as "brush knee and twist step", "step back and whirl arms", "step forward to grasp the peacock's tail" and "fly obliquely" etc. For the posture, it seems that the body is leaning forward while actually, from the head to the heel through the buttocks, the 3 points form a straight line slanting towards the ground which is known as the "upright when slanting".

In footwork, it focuses on stance of the Chinese character "川". Both feet are paralleled with the tips and the heels facing the same direction. The footwork in bow stance requires the knee of the front leg in alignment with the toes. Both feet in bow stance is alike stepping on the edges of the Chinese character "川". The requirement for the footwork in empty stance is also on the character"川"by having the empty foot placed onto the center line of the character. Another characteristic in Wu style Tai Ji Quan is its "horse stance", in another name known as the "pile stance" which other styles of Tai Ji Quan seldom have. Its hand postures emphasize the opening of the "tiger mouth" with the thumb facing upward.

When practicing, try to avoid the movements of leaning the body, folding in the waist and pushing the buttocks out by seeking the"upright when slanting"posture. Don't extend the knees beyond the toes or lift up the heels without keeping the balance between both feet etc.

Methods to overcome such obstacles: Understand the characteristics of Wu style Tai Ji Quan first and after that, add the practice of the single movements and use the guiding signs for training when necessary. For example, the training in footwork of Wu style Tai Ji Quan can be done by drawing 2 parallel lines according to the width of the shoulder and place the feet onto each of the lines. Do the supplementary exercises such as stretching the ankles for accompanying.

5. The competition routine of Sun style Tai Ji Quan

The footwork of the combined advancing and retreating is one of the main characteristics of Sun style Tai Ji Quan. It requires the "follow up step" when advancing and the "draw in step" when retreating just like a worm wriggling and the leaf floating in the water. The routine presents the liveliness when moving, precision in its paces, suitable distance in its steps, lightness and agility in its footwork. When stepping up, move your legs steadily between the emptiness and the solidness with your weight sunk in the center under the crotch. While shifting the weight, keep the body steady without the obvious ups and downs. When the hind leg follows up onto the fore leg, the distance in between is approximately 10 cm and a springing force should also be concealed within the movement. When retreating, relax the waist, sink the crotch down and draw in your leg. The advancing and retreating should be performed like sliding on an arc in the steady and even speed.

During practice, such faults often occur: the hind leg is forced to lift up when stepping forward; when shifting the weight, there's no changes in the internal strength and the landing point is not precise; the distance between both feet is either too close or too far; you may step onto the other foot when turning foot inward and the steps may be drifted without a sunken strength.

Methods to overcome such obstacles:

First, understand the essential character of the footwork. Then, practice the advancing and retreating with the aid of the signs and marks (such as drawing lines on the ground) to limit the distance and the landing points of the steps.

The opening and closing of hands is another important characteristic in the competition routine of Sun style. When opening or closing hands, pay attention to the changes of your chest during the breath with the elbows and the shoulders sunk and prevent the elbows from lifting up or lacking of the internal force and the "Qi".

Methods to overcome such obstacles: Properly understand the essentials of the movement by using the stimulation of the external force, such as the resistant force and the supporting force and the key points of the movement. You can hold a ruler or a stick with the same length as your face and form the opening hands stance to overcome the wrong movements of the hands.

6. The competition routine of 42 style Tai Ji Quan

The competition routine of 42 style is mainly designed for the purpose of competing. It is being standardized in its movements, the positions and the layout. When practicing, you should follow the strict rules and refine every movement. As there are many styles used in this routine, people often get confused on how they should perform these movements. In fact, according to the regulations and the arrangements of the routine, the characteristics of this routine are very similar to that of 48 style Tai Ji Quan which are mainly adopted from Yang style. The movements of other styles are also carried out in the manner of Yang style but remained the original posture of the movements. For example, the movement of "cover and strike fist" taken from Chen style still requires the releasing force but modified in the footwork and hand postures. Another example is the "Jade girl working with shuttles" taken from Wu (吴) style, the body is kept upright instead of keeping it "upright when slanting".

7. The competition routine of 42 style Tai Ji Jian

At present, the competition routine of 42 style Tai Ji Jian is the only weaponry competition style to go along with the competition routine of 42 style Tai Ji Quan. In some competitions the scores for both 42 style Tai Ji Quan and Tai Ji Jian are accumulated and the winner will be given an all-round award. This competition routine of Tai Ji Jian was designed based on the traditional movements of Yang, Wu(吴), and Chen style Tai Ji Jian with more emphasis on Yang style. This competition style shares the similar traits with the competition routine of 42 style Tai Ji Quan and the technical characteristics are as the followings: The posture is elegant with the force penetrated onto the sword and the movements are agile and steady with the well balanced softness and hardness.

The most common difficulty the learners face when practicing this routine is the coordination of the body movements and the ambiguity of the sword movements.

Methods to overcome the obstacles: a) Master the movements of Tai Ji Quan before learning the movements of Tai Ji Jian. You have to master the basics before advancing to the higher levels. Tai Ji Quan is the basis for Tai Ji Jian because the body movements, stances and footwork used in Tai Ji Jian are identical to Tai Ji Quan. You can understand the important techniques of Tai Ji Jian by practicing Tai Ji Quan and apply them to the swordplay. b) Learn the routine systematically and focus on the accuracy in movements. For the beginners, it is crucial to perform every movement precisely according to the key points. The beginners should avoid learning too many movements at a time without fully

understanding the important points of each in case to form the formation of the wrong movements and the bad habits which will be very difficult to correct later. c) Master the movements before practicing your mind and then combine the movements and your mind into one. Tai Ji Jian is the swordplay guided by your mind and the "Qi". However, when you begin to practice the sword, you should first pay attention to the external movements (mainly the regulations of the sword) such as the differences between striking sword and pointing sword and the route of the waving sword etc. The correct external movement is the precondition in using your mind whereas, of course, the form and mind are not completely separated. This is only the different stages of practicing the sword. If the mind is used correctly, it can increase the accuracy of the movements. What we want to achieve at last is to use your mind to guide your sword and to combine both the sword and the mind into one to reaching the high level of unifying the form, mind, spirit and sword into one.